Tokyo University of Science
English Listening and Speaking

Speaking Practice for Presenting in English

Makiko Asaba
浅場 眞紀子

KENKYUSHA

Speaking Practice for Presenting in English

Tokyo University of Science English Listening and Speaking

Copyright © 2019 by Makiko Asaba

PRINTED IN JAPAN

Introduction

Dear Tokyo University of Science first-year students,

Welcome to *Speaking Practice for Presenting in English*.

This textbook is designed to help you become a better speaker of English. Improving your ability to speak another language is like building a brick-and-mortar house. Before you construct the house itself, you need to start with a solid foundation. For the language learner, this foundation is the basic knowledge of grammar, vocabulary, and pronunciation / intonation. You internalize this knowledge through a lot of simple drills and practice until it becomes part of your automatic skill set as an English speaker.

In this era of ever-faster advancing technology and a global economy, being a good user of English is one of the essential qualities of a good scientist, researcher, or business professional. When more than fifty percent of the most frequently visited websites are in English and over eighty percent of academic papers are written in English, it is crucial to be able to use the language proficiently. When you attend an international conference, you will be listening to talks in English, and if you are the speaker, you will certainly be asked to present your views in English.

This textbook begins with a simple self-introduction unit and ends with a five-minute presentation that includes a Q&A session. It is organized in a way that helps you develop your speaking skills step by small step. I hope you enjoy learning and practicing spoken English through the exercises in this textbook. By doing so, you will establish a good foundation for further study and improvement. Practice makes perfect.

Makiko Asaba

How to Use This Textbook

This textbook is a presentation-based textbook designed for all first year *English: Listening and Speaking* students. The main goal of the textbook is to develop students' presentation skills, by presenting and practicing phrases, vocabulary, pronunciation, and planning strategies. It is a compulsory subtextbook for all first year students in the *English: Listening and Speaking* classes. This subtextbook will be used in addition to another textbook which the teacher will choose.

Features of the textbook

The textbook is divided up into 20 units, each with models, guided practice of phrases for presentation and conversation, pronunciation practice, and speaking practice. In Unit 10 and Unit 20 there is a presentation task which all students must do. The presentation tasks in Unit 10 and Unit 20 make use of the presentation skills and phrases which are covered in the units before them.

Using the textbook

It is recommended that around **20 minutes of each class** is spent using this textbook. Teachers are not expected to follow the units and exercises one-by-one in this textbook, but to pick and choose sections which they think will be most useful for their students. In doing this, teachers should always keep in mind the goal of the textbook – to help students develop skills for giving presentations, and make sure that all of the material covered will help students to do the presentation tasks in Unit 10 and Unit 20. We expect teachers to select, skip, adapt, and supplement the material in this textbook as they see fit, in line with the particular levels and contexts of their own classes and teaching styles. For example, lower level classes might find it more helpful to focus more on the *examples and useful expressions*. On the other hand, higher level classes who are already familiar with many of *the useful expressions* might find it more useful to focus on accuracy in the pronunciation, intonation and fluency exercises in the textbook. The key thing to bear in mind is the presentations in Units 10 and 20 that students will have to do. It is recommended that teachers think about these presentation tasks and plan backwards – think what material is needed to cover in Units 1-9 for students to successfully produce a presentation in Unit 10, and similarly Units 11-19 for the presentation in Unit 20.

Presentation tasks (Unit 10 and Unit 20)

The two presentation tasks are compulsory for all students. It is strongly recommended that students do the presentation task in Unit 10 somewhere around the end of the first semester, and the presentation in Unit 20 somewhere around the end of the second semester. These presentations will be assessed by the teachers in class, and will make up 17% of the overall grade for each semester. Teachers are permitted to create their own rubric for grading the presentations of their students. **Students should be informed at the beginning of each semester that they will give a presentation later in the semester, and that it will count towards 17% of the grade.** In classes with large numbers of students, teachers can spread the presentations over 2 classes.

Teachers can adapt the presentation tasks according to their students' needs and level. The topic of the presentations has been left open. It is recommended that teachers specify and narrow down possible areas of topics that students can choose. Here are some suggestions which teachers and students might find useful:

- Presenting about your life as a TUS student

- Presenting about a field within your major subject

- Presenting about an inspirational person

- Presenting about an article / video / book, etc.

- Presenting about research

- An opinion based presentation (i.e. giving a presentation which gives an argument about a potentially controversial topic: the death penalty, refugees in Japan, gay marriage, etc.)

• Teachers' or students' own suggestions

In Unit 20 there is a long list of possible suggestions for activities to practice and prepare presentations on pp.93-94. **These are only suggestions**, and their relevance will depend upon which kind of topic area the presentations are about, and the needs and levels of students.

Teachers should decide in advance which kind of presentation they will be doing so as to guide the selection of material to cover. For example, while Unit 18 on 'Explaining Graphs, Charts, and Table 1' and Unit 19 on 'Explaining Graphs, Charts and Tables 2' might be very useful for students giving a presentation about research, or on an article or book with some sort of statistical information in, it is probably not particularly useful for students giving a presentation about their lives as TUS students. If teachers would like students to give opinion based presentations, then more time should be given to Unit 15 on 'Pros and Cons'. If teachers wish to emphasize the interactivity in presentations in question and answer sections of presentations, then Unit 14 on 'Agreeing and Disagreeing' will be useful. **Only the units and the sections which will best help students complete the presentation tasks need to be covered in the class.**

We would like to express our gratitude to the author, Makiko Asaba, who developed this textbook especially for TUS students. Our gratitude also goes to Yasushi Kaneko of Kenkyusha who helped and guided us throughout the process of making this textbook.

Makoto Shimizu
Yukimitsu Namiki
Shin-ichi Kitada
Ryoko Harikae
William Simpson

Contents

Notes

Main Objective: The main speech function to practice.

Advanced Objective: A slightly more complex speech function than the main objective.

Target Grammar: The grammar elements to be used to fulfill the purpose of the speech.

Target Expressions: The expressions and phrases to learn and use.

Target WPM: Words per minute, a suggested minimum number of words in students' speech per minute. The example passage in each unit represents the unit's target speech speed. However, depending on students' speaking ability, this should be flexible.

Shadowing: Practice repeating after the speaker as soon as possible. Don't wait and listen to the whole sentence, but repeat what you heard as soon as possible. Pay attention to rhythm, intonation and pronunciation.

Overlapping: Practice reading out loud with the speaker. Try and read exactly the same word as the speaker is reading. Pay attention to fluency.

Unit | 1

Introductions

- **Main Objective:** Introduce yourself to others
- **Advanced Objective:** Introduce one person to others

- **Target Grammar:** Be verb
- **Target Expressions:** I'm from ~. / My major is ~.
- **Target WPM:** 30

Vocabulary

☐ freshman　1 年生・新入生　☐ sophomore　2 年生　☐ junior　3 年生　☐ senior　4 年生　☐ major　専攻　☐ faculty of science　理学部　☐ mathematics　数学　☐ physics　物理学　☐ chemistry　化学　☐ applied　応用の　☐ undergraduate　学部生　☐ graduate school　大学院　☐ graduate student　大学院生　☐ computer science　コンピューターサイエンス

DOWNLOAD 01

Example

My name is Takuya Honda. T-A-K-U-Y-A, Takuya. Please call me Tak.
I'm from Japan. I'm a freshman at Tokyo University of Science. My major is applied chemistry. Nice to meet you.

Shadowing and Overlapping

For self-study or in-class practice, listen to the audio, do shadowing and overlapping of the example. Practice the passage until you can say it smoothly.

Create Your Own

① My name is _____.

② Please call me _____

_____ .

③ I'm from _____

_____ .

④ I'm a _____

_____ at Tokyo University of Science.

⑤ My major is _____

_____ .

⑥ Nice to meet you.

🧠 | Training

Step 1: Fill in the blanks above.

Step 2: Practice reading your sentences out loud.

Step 3: Practice speaking without looking at what you wrote. If you forget, it is OK
to glance at what you wrote. Practice until you can say it without stopping.

Step 4: Make groups of three or four students.

Step 5: Introduce yourself to your group.

Memo

Advanced Practice 1: Introducing others

Work with a partner. Take turns introducing yourselves to each other. When it is your partner's turn, take notes about what he / she says. Finally, introduce your partner to the other members of your group.

Advanced Practice 2: Speak more

Now that you have practiced introducing yourself several times, add two additional details. Put the details between ⑤ and ⑥ .

_____

_____

_____

_____

DOWNLOAD 02

Pronunciation Tips: Liaison

Listen and copy what your teacher does.

★ My name‿is
★ I'm‿a freshman‿a(t) Tokyo University of Science

Extra Activity: How many sentences can you say in one minute?

Make pairs. Student A speaks for one minute about himself / herself. Student B counts the number of sentences his / her partner says. After one minute, switch roles.

The student who says the most sentences wins the game.

Memo

Presentation Skills + Useful Expressions

Greetings and Self-introduction

At the beginning of your presentation, you should greet the audience and introduce yourself and your peers (if it is a group presentation).

◆ **Useful Expressions**

1. Hello everyone.
   Good morning everyone. / Good afternoon everyone.

2. Welcome to (my / our) presentation.
   Thank you for coming to (my / our) presentation today.

3. I'm Ryo Tanaka. I'm a freshman in applied chemistry. And (here is my team, / here are my team members,) Aya Saito, Ken Tanaka, and Kei Suzuki.

Unit | 2

Daily Routine

- **Main Objective:** Talk about your daily routine and give some details
- **Advanced Objective:** Talk about others' routine activities and give some details

- **Target Grammar:** Present tense verb with frequency adverbs
- **Target Expressions:** I usually ~. / I sometimes ~.
- **Target WPM:** 30

Vocabulary

□ routine　日課・定期的な行動や活動　　□ lab (laboratory)　研究室　実験室　　□ get to ~　～に着く　　□ stop by ~　～に立ち寄る　　□ have a class　授業がある　　□ check out books（図書館で）本を借りる　　□ write a paper　論文（レポート）を書く　　□ a part-time job　アルバイト　　□ go out for lunch　昼食を（外に）食べに行く

DOWNLOAD 03

Example

I usually get to campus around 8:30 in the morning. First, I stop by my lab to check some data. Then I attend class in first and second periods. After that, I eat lunch in the cafeteria.

👤 | Shadowing and Overlapping

For self-study or in-class practice, listen to the audio, do shadowing and overlapping of the example. Practice the passage until you can say it smoothly.

📝 | Create Your Own

① I usually _____.

② First, I _____.

③ Then I _____.

④ After that / After -ing, I _____.

⑤ _____.

🔊 | Training

Step 1: Fill in the blanks above.

Step 2: Practice reading your sentences out loud.

Step 3: Practice speaking without looking at what you wrote. If you forget, it is OK to glance at what you wrote. Practice until you can say it without stopping.

Step 4: Make groups of three or four students.

Step 5: Describe your daily routine to your group.

Memo

👥 | Advanced Practice 1: Using timeline expressions

Work with a partner. Take turns talking about your routine activities using some of the timeline expressions listed below to clearly show the order of the activities. Each speaker should keep talking for at least one minute.

> **at ~ o'clock / in the morning / at noon / in the afternoon / in the evening / then / after that / after -ing / before / next / first / second / third / finally**

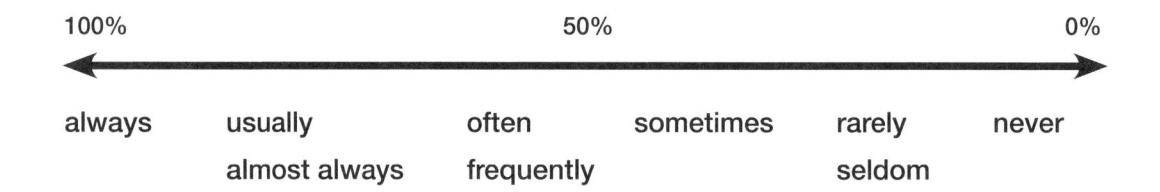

Advanced Practice 2: Talking with frequency adverbs

100%			50%			0%

← →

always	usually		often	sometimes	rarely	never
	almost always		frequently		seldom	

Make pairs.

Student A: Ask as many questions as you can in one minute

What do you (always / usually / often) do?

How often do you ~?

Student B: Answer questions by simply using "I + a frequency adverb + a verb"

I always ... / I usually ... / I often ... / I never ..., etc.

DOWNLOAD 04

Pronunciation Tips: p, t, k

Listen and copy what your teacher does.

Unlike Japanese, many of English sounds require greater breath force, especially /p/, /t/, /k/. When one of these sounds is at the beginning of a word and in a stressed syllable, it has a strong aspiration. Example: paper, teacher, campus

When these sounds are at the end of a word, it becomes much weaker. Do not insert an extra vowel when a word is ending with a consonant.

Example: stop → stop<u>pu</u> × Katakana pronunciation

Listen and practice the following list of words.

pit, pet, pie, paper
tie, tip, toe, teacher
cat, cap, cake, campus

Make pairs. Student A speaks for one minute about his / her daily routine. Student B counts the number of verbs his / her partner speaks. The student who says the most verbs wins the game.

Presentation Skills + Useful Expressions

When you give a presentation, it is important to tell the audience the purpose of the presentation right at the beginning. This lets the audience know what to expect from the presentation. A good place to say the purpose of the presentation is right after you introduce yourself.

◆ **Useful Expressions**

1. The purpose of (my / our) presentation is to share our research results on

   _____.

2. Today, (I'm / we're) here to talk about our research method for

   _____.

3. Today, (I'd / we'd) like to discuss various issues related to

   _____

   _____.

Unit | 3

Talking about the Past

- **Main Objective:** Talk about your past activities and events
- **Advanced Objective:** Talk about your past activities and events and give details

- **Target Grammar:** Past tense verb / Present perfect
- **Target Expressions:** I learned ~. / I've ~.
- **Target WPM:** 30

Vocabulary

□ **become interested in ~** 〜に興味を持つようになる   □ **biography** 伝記
□ **encourage** 〜を励ます   □ **inspire** 心を動かす、鼓舞する   □ **Einstein** アルバート・アインシュタイン (1879-1955)   □ **latest** 最新の   □ **modern** 現代の   □ **theory** 理論
□ **relativity** 相対性   □ **theory of relativity** 相対性理論

DOWNLOAD 05

Example

I became interested in science when I was ten years old. I read a biography of Einstein for a school report. His story inspired me. Since then, I've read many books about famous scientists.

👤 | Shadowing and Overlapping

For self-study or in-class practice, listen to the audio, do shadowing and overlapping of the example. Practice the passage until you can say it smoothly.

📝 | Create Your Own

① I became interested in science when I _____ .

② (What happened?) _____ .

③ (What did you do?) _____.

④ (How did you feel?) _____.

⑤ _____.

Training

Step 1: Fill in the blanks above.

Step 2: Practice reading your sentences out loud.

Step 3: Practice speaking without looking at what you wrote. If you forget, it is OK to glance at what you wrote. Practice until you can say it without stopping.

Step 4: Make groups of three or four students.

Step 5: Share your past experience with your group.

Memo

Advanced Practice 1: Using time expression

Make pairs. Take turns talking about your past activities and experiences in chronological order using past tense and present perfect tense (Refer to some of the expressions in the box below). You should be talking continuously for at least one minute.

For past tense:
when I was __ years old / in 2015 / after __ / last month / last week / yesterday
For present perfect:
I've ~ since ~ / I've ~ for ~

Advanced Practice 2: Telling your life history

Make pairs.

Student A: Ask as many questions as possible about Student B's life using past and present perfect
What did you do (when you were ~)?
What did you enjoy doing (when you were ~)?
Have you ever ~ ?
What have you ~?

Student B: Answer questions with
(When I was ~,) I often ~.
I've ~.

Presentation Skills + Useful Expressions

(See "How to use this textbook")

After talking about the purpose of your presentation, you should state the outline. It shows how many parts your speech contains. It works as a map that shows the route and the goals of your presentation. The audience can understand your presentation much better if you share the outline at the beginning.

◆ **Useful Expressions: Outline 1**

---

1. Let's look at the outline. / Please look at the outline today.

2. Here is what (I'm / we're) going to (discuss / talk) about in (my / our) presentation.

3. As you can see, (I / we) have divided my presentation into three parts.

4. First, _____.

   Second, _____.

   Finally, _____.

Memo

Unit | 4

Future Plans

- **Main Objective:** Talk about your future plans and events
- **Advanced Objective:** Talk about your future plans and events with details

- **Target Grammar:** Future verb
- **Target Expressions:** I will ~ / I'm going to ~ / I'm planning to ~ / I'm -ing
- **Target WPM:** 30 ~ 35

Vocabulary

☐ theoretical physicist　理論物理学者　　☐ theoretical physics　理論物理学
☐ astrophysics　宇宙物理学　　☐ be attracted to ~　〜に惹かれる、魅了される　　☐ space /
the universe　宇宙　　☐ discover　〜を発見する　　☐ secret　秘密、秘密の　　☐ get a job
仕事を手に入れる　　☐ I've always -ed　ずっと〜していた　　☐ work as ~　〜（職種）として働
く（ex. work as a programmer）

DOWNLOAD 06

Example

In the future, I want to become a theoretical physicist. I'm planning to study astrophysics in graduate school. I've always been interested in space, so my dream is to get a job at NASA.

👤 | Shadowing and Overlapping

For self-study or in-class practice, listen to the audio, do shadowing and overlapping of the example. Practice the passage until you can say it smoothly.

📝 | Create Your Own

① In the future, I want to_____.

② (What will you do?) _____.

③ (Why?) _____.

④ (How will you feel?) _____.

⑤ _____.

Grammar: Discuss differences in will / be going to / be -ing

Training

Step 1: Fill in the blanks above.

Step 2: Practice reading your sentences out loud.

Step 3: Practice speaking without looking at what you wrote. If you forget, it is OK to glance at what you wrote. Practice until you can say it without stopping.

Step 4: Make groups of three or four students.

Step 5: Tell your group about something you plan to do in the future.

Memo

Advanced Practice 1: Using time expressions

Make pairs. Take turns talking about your future plans and dreams using the future tense and the expressions listed below. Keep talking for at least one minute.

> I will ~ / I'm going to ~ / I'm planning to ~ / I want to ~ / I'd like to ~ / I need to ~ / I have to ~
>
> next year / in the future / after I graduate / three years from now / in 2025
>
> ★ If I can ~ / I will ~ (First conditional)

Advanced Practice 2: Your future plans

Make pairs.

Student A: Ask as many questions as possible about Student B's future plans and dreams

What are your dreams?

What will you do (when ~ / after ~) ?

What are you planning to do (when ~ / in five years from now) ?

Student B: Answer questions with

I will ~ / I will be ~

I'm going to ~ / I'm planning to ~ / I'm -ing

Presentation Skills + Useful Expressions

Your presentation outline should include how long your speech will last. In addition, it is important to tell the audience when it is OK for them to ask questions.

◆ Useful Expressions: Outline 2

1. My presentation will last about 15 minutes. / I'll be speaking for about 15 minutes.

2. There will be a question and answer session at the end of the presentation.

3. If you have any questions, please hold them until the end.

4. If you have any questions, please feel free to ask them at any time during my presentation.

Memo

Unit | 5

Describing People

- **Main Objective:** Talk about people you know
- **Advanced Objective:** Talk about a famous person

- **Target Grammar:** Be verb + adjective / third person singular
- **Target Expressions:** My professor is very ~. He / She enjoys ~.
- **Target WPM:** 40

Vocabulary

☐ **smart** 頭がよい　　☐ **funny** おもしろい　　☐ **tell jokes** 冗談を言う　　☐ **respect** 尊敬する　　☐ **make (a person) laugh** （人）を笑わせる　　☐ **He / she is in his / her ~'s** （30's, 40's, 50's, etc.）彼・彼女は〜代です（年齢）　　☐ **shy** 恥ずかしがりな　　☐ **mean** 意地悪な　　☐ **outgoing** 外向的な　　☐ **hard-working** 仕事・勉強熱心な　　☐ **energetic** 活動的な・元気な

 DOWNLOAD 07

Example

Professor Sato is my math professor. I think he's in his 40's. He's smart and funny. I really enjoy his class because he always tells jokes and makes us laugh. Professor Sato is also a pianist. I respect him a lot because he's so talented.

👤 | Shadowing and Overlapping

For self-study or in-class practice, listen to the audio, do shadowing and overlapping of the example. Practice the passage until you can say it smoothly.

📝 | Create Your Own

① (A person's name) is _____ .

② (He / She) is _____

_____

_____ .

for ② describe the person's (1. personality, 2. physical appearance, 3. what he / she does), etc.

③ _____

_____

_____ .

for ③ in order to support what you wrote in ② , introduce an episode in past tense or present tense (routine)

④ I (like / respect / admire) him / her _____

because _____ .

🔊 | Training

Step 1: Fill in the blanks above.

Step 2: Practice reading your sentences out loud.

Step 3: Practice speaking without looking at what you wrote. If you forget, it is OK to glance at what you wrote. Practice until you can say it without stopping.

Step 4: Make groups of three or four students.

Step 5: Tell your group about the famous person you chose.

_____

_____

 **Advanced Practice 1: Talking about a famous person**

Make pairs. Take turns introducing a famous person you know to your partner. When it is your partner's turn, take notes about what he / she says.

_____

_____

_____

_____

_____

_____

_____

_____.

Advanced Practice 2: Adding more details

Now that you have practiced describing someone several times. Add additional details to your speech. Keep speaking for more than one minute. Add details, such as the person's physical appearance and the clothes they typically wear.

Extra Activity: Guess who?

Work in small groups. One student talks about someone famous (a historical figure or a celebrity) without saying the person's name. The other students guess who the person is. The speaker has to keep talking until someone gets the right answer.

Presentation Skills + Useful Expressions

It is good to learn some typical expressions for telling the audience what you are going to speak about at the beginning of your presentation. Telling the audience what you are about to talk about prepares them for your message, and makes it easier for them to understand you. Use one of the expressions below.

◆ **Useful Expressions:**

---

1. I'm going to start with ~.

2. Let me start by -ing ~.

3. I'd like to begin my presentation by -ing ~.

*explaining / introducing / describing / showing, etc.

Memo

Unit | 6

Describing Places

- **Main Objective:** Talk about a place you like
- **Advanced Objective:** Talk about a place you want to visit

- **Target Grammar:** Be verb + preposition / passive
- **Target Expressions:** My campus is in ~. / It's located in ~.
- **Target WPM:** 40

Vocabulary

□ campus　キャンパス　　□ metropolitan area　首都圏　　□ mainly　主に　　□ be located in / at ~　　〜に位置している　　□ in the heart of ~　〜の中心部に　　□ be surrounded by ~　〜に囲まれている　　□ suburb　郊外　　□ campus bookstore　大学生協書籍部　□ faculty　学部、学部教員陣

DOWNLOAD 08

| Example |

Let me introduce my university.

TUS has campuses in Kagurazaka, Noda, Katsushika and Oshamanbe. Three are in the Tokyo metropolitan area, but one is in Hokkaido. I study mainly at the Kagurazaka campus. It's located in the heart of Tokyo and surrounded by many shops and restaurants.

👤 | Shadowing and Overlapping

For self-study or in-class practice, listen to the audio, do shadowing and overlapping of the example. Practice the passage until you can say it smoothly.

✎ | Create Your Own

① Let me introduce (name of a place / location) _____ .

② (Give a general description of the place)

It's _____ .

③ (Describe the place more in detail)

_____ .

④ (Talk about [what you do / what you enjoy doing there])

_____

_____ .

♪ | Training

Step 1: Fill in the blanks above.

Step 2: Practice reading your sentences out loud.

Step 3: Practice speaking without looking at what you wrote. If you forget, it is OK to glance at what you wrote. Practice until you can say it without stopping.

Step 4: Make groups of three or four students.

Step 5: Choose a (place / location), and introduce it to your group.

Memo

 **Advanced Practice 1: Talking about a place you want to visit**

Work with a partner. Take turns introducing a place you want to visit in the future. When it is your partner's turn, take notes about what he / she says.

Use the following expressions to talk about your hopes and wishes:

I'd (like / love) to visit ~.
If I could (go to / visit) ~, I would ~.

Advanced Practice 2: Summarizing and re-introducing

Work with a partner. While Student A speaks about a place, Student B listens and takes notes. After Student A finishes speaking, Student B summarizes what Student A said. Student A gives feedback to Student B about any missing or incorrect information. Switch roles.

 DOWNLOAD 09

Pronunciation Tips: L and R

Listen and copy the audio or what your teacher does.

Let me introduce my university.
TUS has campuses in Kagurazaka, Noda, Katsushika and Oshamanbe. Three are in the Tokyo metropolitan area, but one is in Hokkaido. I study mainly at the Kagurazaka campus. It's located in the heart of Tokyo and surrounded by many shops and restaurants.

Although it is often difficult for Japanese learners to hear the difference between L and R, they are completely different phonemes in English. L and R even look different. Use a mirror and check your mouth. Find words that contain L and / or R in the passage.

R: Your tongue is touching nowhere inside your mouth. It is pronounced often with lip rounding.

L: No lip rounding. Air comes out from both sides of the tongue. From the front, you can see the back of your tongue.

Practice the words in the passage.
let / mainly / locate / area / restaurant

Extra Activity: Talking about a famous place

Work in small groups. One student talks about somewhere famous or well-known (a place that most students have basic knowledge of) without saying the name of the place. The other students guess what the place is. The speaker has to keep describing the place until someone gets the right answer.

Presentation Skills + Useful Expressions

Signposting expressions are words that help the audience follow the flow of your presentation. For example, if you say, "For example," they know that the next you say is an example of the point you just mentioned.

◆ Useful Expressions

> 1. Ordering: First, / Firstly, / Second, / Next, / Finally,
>
> 2. Giving an example: For example, / For instance,
>
> 3. Making a similar point: In addition, / Moreover, / What's more,
>
> 4. Acknowledging another point of view: While, ... / On the one hand, ...
>   On the other hand, ...

Unit | 7

Asking Questions

- **Main Objective:** Become able to ask various questions
- **Advanced Objective:** Become able to ask and answer more than ten
  questions in pairwork in one minute

- **Target Grammar:** Question forms
- **Target Expressions:** Yes / No questions: Is it ~? / Have you ever ~?, etc.
- **Open Questions:** What is ~? / How are ~?, / Why did ~?, etc.
- **Target WPM:** 40

Vocabulary

□ **quality** 特徴　□ **ability** 能力　□ **work out** （解答を）出す　□ **complex** 複雑な
□ **equation** 方程式　□ **opinion** 意見　□ **effective** 効果的な　□ **Have you ever ~?**
〜をしたことありますか？　□ **invention** 発明　□ **reliable** 信頼できる

DOWNLOAD 10

Example

Have you ever thought about what the most important quality for a scientist is? Is it the ability to work out complex equations? Or is it the ability to write computer programs? My opinion is very simple. I think it is the ability to ask insightful questions.

Shadowing and Overlapping

For self-study or in-class practice, listen to the audio, do shadowing and overlapping of the example. Practice the passage until you can say it smoothly.

Create Your Own

① Have you ever thought about what _____ is?

_____ .

② Is it _____ ?

③ Or is it _____ ?

④ (In my opinion, / I think) it is _____ .

⑤ What do you think ? _____

_____ .

Training

Step 1: Fill in the blanks above.

Step 2: Practice reading your sentences out loud.

Step 3: Practice speaking without looking at what you wrote. If you forget, it is OK to glance at what you wrote. Practice until you can say it without stopping.

Step 4: Make groups of three or four students.

Step 5: Say the passage you created above in front of your group without reading the text.

Advanced Practice 1: Asking as many questions as possible in one minute

Work with a partner. Student A asks as many questions as possible to Student B. Student B answers each question as briefly as possible*. Student A keeps asking questions for one minute and Student B counts the number of questions while answering them. Try to ask and answer more than eight questions in one minute.

For Yes / No questions, answer only "Yes." or "No."
For What / When / Who / Where questions, answer with a word or a short phrase.
For Why / How (open) questions, answer with short sentences.

🗣 | Advanced Practice 2: Roleplay

Student A is the owner of a shop. Student B is an applicant for a part-time job at Student A's shop. Student A interviews Student B. Student A asks questions and decides whether or not to hire Student B. Next, Student A and Student B switch roles.

🗣 | Pronunciation Tips: Weak vowels

Listen to the teacher read the passage. Find weak syllables and function words that contain weak vowels.

> Have you ever thought about what the most important quality for a scientist is? Is it the ability to work out complex equations? Or is it the ability to write computer programs? My opinion is very simple. I think it is the ability to ask insightful questions.

★ Schwa /ə/ weak vowel

The schwa sound exists everywhere in English and helps create rhythm and intonation that characterize English. Schwa is actually the most frequent vowel in English speech. It occurs in unstressed syllables in words and also in function words.

What does schwa sound like? Ask your teacher to demonstrate, or search for "schwa" on the Internet. Also, look up a dictionary and find /ə/ in phonetic symbols.

Examples:
about = əbout / the = thə / as a = əzə / important = importən(t) / ability = əbility

Extra Activity: Searching for an answer

The length of this activity is up to the teacher.

Think of one question to ask your classmates. The question should be something you don't know the answer to, but you want to know.

All students stand up. Walk around the classroom and ask the question to each student until you find a person who knows the answer.

Your question: _____

_____.

Presentation Skills + Useful Expressions

When you give a presentation, sometimes it is necessary to summarize what you have mentioned to help and enhance the audience's understanding. It is a good idea to summarize the content at the end of your presentation or even at the end of every part.

Practice summarizing what you talked about in the body of your speech. This is to refresh the audience's memory and make sure that what you want to achieve with your presentation is clear to them.

◆ Useful Expressions

> **1.** In my presentation, first, I talked about …
>
> **2.** Second, I (mentioned / discussed / showed) …
>
> **3.** And finally, I (spoke about / addressed / explained) …

Unit | 8

Making Requests

- **Main Objective:** Make informal requests
- **Advanced Objective:** Make polite requests

- **Target Grammar:** Auxiliary verbs
- **Target Expressions:** Could you ~? / Could you possibly ~? / Do you think you could ~?
- **Target WPM:** 50

Vocabulary

☐ semester　学期　　☐ apply　応募する　　☐ experience　経験、体験、経験する
☐ helpful　助かる、役に立つ　　☐ ..., right?　〜ですよね？　　☐ could　can の過去形だが、丁寧な依頼をする時にも使う　　☐ would　will の過去形だが、仮定の話や丁寧な話をする時にも使う
☐ what it is like ~　どのような様子か、どのようなものか　　☐ Could you possibly ~?　〜はできますでしょうか? Could you ~? よりも丁寧　　☐ Do you think you could ~?　〜はできると思われますか? Could you ~? よりも間接的で丁寧　　☐ gist　要点

DOWNLOAD 12

Example

Could you meet me after class today? You studied in Canada for one semester, right? I'm thinking about applying to study there, too. If you could tell me about your experience, that would be really helpful for me. I'd like to know what it was like to live there, and what your classes were like.

👤💬 | Shadowing and Overlapping

For self-study or in-class practice, listen to the audio, do shadowing and overlapping of the example. Practice the passage until you can say it smoothly.

✐ | Create Your Own

Imagine a situation where you are making a request to someone.

① Could you _____ ?

② (Explain why you are making a request to that person)

   _____ .

③ I'm thinking about _____

   _____ .

④ So if you could _____, it would be really helpful for me.

⑤ (If you have anything to add) _____ .

🗣 | Training

Step 1: Fill in the blanks above.

Step 2: Practice reading your sentences out loud.

Step 3: Practice speaking without looking at what you wrote. If you forget, it is OK
to glance at what you wrote. Practice until you can say it without stopping.

Step 4: Make pairs.

Step 5: Practice speaking your passage with your partner.

Memo

Advanced Practice 1: Making it more polite

To make your passage more polite, start sentence ① on p. 39 with one of the expressions below. Practice your own passage or the example passage using these expressions that are more polite.

> Could you possibly ~?
> Do you think you could ~?
> Would it be possible for you to ~?

Think of other ways and / or expressions to make your requests more polite. Share your ideas with the class.

Advanced Practice 2: Roleplay

Now that you have practiced making requests several times, make pairs and do a roleplay. Student A makes a request based on his / her passage. Student B practices both accepting the request and turning down the request.

◆ **Accepting**
Student A: <Make a request>
Student B: Sure. I'd be happy to help.
Student A: Thank you.

◆ **Turning down**
Student A: <Make a request>
Student B: I'd like to, but I can't. <Give a reason>
Student A: OK. Thanks anyway.

Pronunciation Tips: Linking sound with y

Listen and copy what your teacher does.

Could_you, Would_you, Did_you, Can_you, Will_you, If_you

Create a sentence using one of above expressions and practice saying.

_____.

Presentation Skills + Useful Expressions

Before you finish, emphasize the purpose of the presentation and thank the audience. It is a good idea to remind the audience once again about the main points of the presentation so that they can clearly remember what you discussed. Also, do not finish your presentation just by saying "That's all.", which is very common among Japanese speakers. However, make sure that you thank the audience for their time.

◆ Useful Expressions

1. In closing, I'd like to stress ....
   Before I finish, I'd like to encourage you to ...
   Now, I hope it's clear to you that ...
   Now, I believe (you / we) can ....

2. Thank you for your (attention / time).
   Thank you for joining (me / us) today.
   Thank you for (coming to / attending) (my / our) presentation today.

Unit | 9

Preferences

- **Main Objective:** Talk about your preferences and give reasons
- **Advanced Objective:** Use the first conditional* to talk about an imaginary situation to support your preferences

*first conditional: If I + past tense verb (or were), I would / could ~.

- **Target Grammar:** First conditional
- **Target Expressions:** I'd prefer to ~. / If I + past tense verb (or were), I would / could ~.
- **Target WPM:** 50+

Vocabulary

□ **prefer** 好む   □ **apartment** アパート、マンション   □ **currently** 現在、今
□ **however** しかしながら（副詞）   □ **rush hour** ラッシュアワー   □ **dislike** 嫌う
□ **ride** 乗る   □ **crowded** 混んでいる   □ **on time** 時間通りに   □ **actually** 実は、実際には   □ **If I were rich, ...** もしお金持ちだったら、…のに

DOWNLOAD 14

Example

I'd prefer to live in an apartment near campus. Currently, I live about an hour from campus by train. However, it takes longer during rush hour and I dislike riding crowded trains. If I lived near school, I could wake up right before class and still get to school on time. So I'd like to move near campus.

👤 | Shadowing and Overlapping

For self-study or in-class practice, listen to the audio, do shadowing and overlapping of the example. Practice the passage until you can say it smoothly.

✍ | Create Your Own

① I'd prefer / I like _____ .

② Explain (background / reasons why you like something) — If you skip ③ , state three or more reasons to support your preference

_____

_____

_____ .

③ Optional — Use first conditional to talk about an imaginary situation

If I _____ ,

I (would / could) _____ .

④ Conclusion — Repeat what you wrote in ① , but change the wording if possible

So, I_____ .

🎧 | Training

Step 1: Fill in the blanks above.

Step 2: Practice reading your sentences out loud.

Step 3: Practice speaking without looking at what you wrote. If you forget, it is OK to glance at what you wrote. Practice until you can say it without stopping.

Step 4: Make groups of three or four students.

Step 5: Say your passage in front of your group. Do not read the text.

Advanced Practice : Imaginary situation

1. If I had one million yen for myself, I (would / could) _____

   _____.

2. If I could get an internship at _____,

   I (would / could) _____

   _____.

3. If I _____,

   I (would / could) _____.

DOWNLOAD 15

Pronunciation Tips: Fall-rise intonation

Fall-rise intonation is commonly used when you want to create and emphasize a chunk of meaning separate from the rest of the sentence. Rise intonation indicates continuation of an utterance or a sentence.

Listen to the audio and practice fall-rise intonation with the following expressions in the example passage.

Listen and copy what your teacher does.

Currently, / However, / If I lived near school, / So,

Presentation Skills + Useful Expressions

Conducting Q&A sessions

One of the most challenging parts of a presentation is the Q&A session. In order to manage this final part of a presentation smoothly, speakers should be familiar with some typical expressions used in this part.

◆ **Useful Expressions**

1. Now, we'll have a Q&A session for about 15 minutes.

2. Does anyone have any questions?
   Now, if you have any questions, (I'd / I'll) be happy to answer them.

3. I'm sorry, but could you repeat your question?
   I'm sorry, I don't follow you. Could you say that again, please?
   I think you are asking about ... Is that right?

4. Thank you. That's a good point.
   Thank you for sharing your question with us.
   Any other questions?
   I can take one last question.
   I'm sorry, but that's all the time we have.

In Unit 10, you are going to review Units 1-9 and also make a short presentation about something you like. Decide what you are going to talk about and bring the thing itself or a photograph of the (item / person / place).

When you give your presentation, show it to your class.

Examples: A photograph of your old house, a photograph of your friend, clothes, ... anything!

Memo

Unit | 10

Review of Units 1-9

- **In this unit you will review the main topics covered in Units 1-9**
- **Review of Units 1-4:** Narration - Talking about yourself

- **Routine:** Present tense (Units 1-2)
- **Events in past:** Past tense (Unit 3)
- **Future plans and dreams:** Future tense (Unit 4)

DOWNLOAD 16

Example

(Present)

My name is Takuya Honda. I'm a freshman at Tokyo University of Science. My major is physics. I usually get to campus around 8:30 in the morning.

(Past)

I became interested in science when I was ten years old. I read a biography of Einstein for a school report.

(Future)

In the future, I want to become a theoretical physicist.

✎ | Create Your Own

(Present) Write sentences describing your routine.

_____

_____

_____

(Past) Write sentences describing your past.

_____

_____

(Future) Write sentences describing your future plans / dreams.

_____

_____

Review of Units 5-6: Describing

Choose words and fill in the blanks in the passage.

When you describe a person, a place or an object, describe it from many

_____ perspectives. _____ details and _____ personal memories and

_____ to make it memorable.

stories,   different,   your,   add

Review of Unit 7: Asking questions

If you were to interview your favorite celebrity, what would you ask?
Create questions using the prompts.

Name of your favorite celebrity: _____

(Are / Were) you _____?

Have you ever _____?

Who _____ ?

Where _____ ?

Why _____ ?

Review of Unit 8: Making polite requests

Make the following request more polite. See the example. Come up with two additional ways to make the request more polite.

<u>Can you help me finish writing my report?</u>

Example: Could you help me finish writing my report?

1. _____ ?

2. _____ ?

Review of Unit 9: Preferences + Short show and tell presentation

Give a short 'Show and Tell' presentation. Use Useful Expressions introduced in the Presentation Skills Sections to organize your speech.

Self-Introduction (Unit 1)
Purpose of the presentation (Unit 2)
Outline 1-2 (Units 3-4)
Beginning (Unit 5)
Signposting (Unit 6)
Summarizing (Unit 7)
Thanking the audience (Unit 8)
*Q&A session (Unit 9) optional

Presentation

Title: _____

Introduction:

Purpose:

Outline:

Body:

Conclusion:

Thank the audience:

*Q&A:

Unit | 11

Recommendations

- **Main Objective:** Make recommendations with reasons
- **Advanced Objective:** Make recommendations politely with reasons
- **Target Expressions:** Why don't you ~? / How about -ing? / I think you should ~.
  / You might want to ~. / It might be a good idea to ~.
- **Target WPM:** 50+

Vocabulary

□ **repeat a year** 留年する　　□ **strict** 厳しい　　□ **keep up with** ついていく　　□ **end up -ing** ～する結果となる　　□ **fail** 落第する、不合格になる　　□ **study group** 自習グループ　　□ **be aware ~** ～と認識する、理解する（命令形の場合注意喚起の意味）　　□ **take A seriously** Aを真剣に考える、Aを真面目にやっている　　□ **elaborate on A** Aについてより詳細に、深く検証する　　□ **summarize** 今までの内容をまとめる　　□ **recap** 簡単に要点をまとめる

 DOWNLOAD 17

Example

I think you should study hard if you don't want to repeat a year. This university is well-known for being very strict. Students who don't keep up with their courses end up failing them. If you're having difficulties, why don't you join our study group? Just be aware that we all take studying seriously.

Shadowing and Overlapping

For self-study or in-class practice, listen to the audio, do shadowing and overlapping of the example. Practice the passage until you can say it smoothly.

✐ | Create Your Own

① I think (you / I / we) should _____ .

② (Explain why you think so)

_____

_____ .

③ (Optional — Use first conditional to talk about an imaginary situation)

If I _____ ,

I (would / could) _____

_____ .

④ (Repeat your recommendation as conclusion)

So, (why don't you / how about) _____

_____ ?

Sample Topics

Recommending your club activities, hobby, a way of doing things, something good for one's health, how to study, how to find a good part-time job, etc.

🗣 | Training

Step 1: Fill in the blanks above.

Step 2: Practice reading your sentences out loud.

Step 3: Practice speaking without looking at what you wrote. If you forget, it is OK to glance at what you wrote.

Step 4: Make groups of three or four students.

Step 5: Say your passage in front of your group. Do not read the text.

Advanced Practice 1: Making politer recommendations

Imagine that you are talking with someone senior to you. Use expressions A, B, and C in the box below to make each of the following sentences 1 to 3 more polite. Make three different polite expressions using the underlined part.

A - (You / We) might want to ~.

B - It might be a good idea [for you / us] to ~.

C - I was wondering if (you / we) could ~.

Ex. Please explain your idea.

A - You might want to explain your idea.

B - It might be a good idea for you to explain your idea.

C - I was wondering if you could explain your idea.

1. We should leave early today.

2. Why don't you talk to Professor Sato?

3. Let's discuss our presentation topics.

Advanced Practice 2: Roleplay

Step 1: Make a list of 2-3 things that you need recommendations from others about.

Step 2: Student A asks Student B about one of the items in his / her list.

Step 3: Student B makes recommendations based on his / her experience.

Step 4: Take turns asking for and giving recommendations.

★ **Signposting expressions**

In Unit 6, we practiced some signposting expressions. Here are other signposting expressions that help your audience by informing them when you move to a new topic. Practice the following expressions and use them in your presentations.

◆ **Useful Expressions**

---

1. Let me move on to the next (topic / point).

2. Let me go back to ~

3. Let me elaborate on ~

4. Let me summarize ~ / To summarize, ~

5. Let me recap ~ / To recap,

6. In conclusion, / To conclude,

Unit | 12

Working with Numbers

- **Main Objective:** Use numbers smoothly in conversation
- **Advanced Objective:** Use large numbers smoothly in conversation
- **Target Expressions:**
    - Use singular number labels. For example, "2,000" is "two thousand," not "two thousands."
    - Do not use "and" to connect millions and thousands, or thousands and hundreds. 1, 234, 500 → One million two hundred thirty four thousand five hundred
    - Using "and" to connect hundreds and tens is optional.
    - Years starting with "20" can be read as, "twenty ..." or "two thousand ..." For example, 2020 can be read "twenty twenty" or "two thousand twenty."
    - Five-figure numbers 10,000-99,999 / six-figure numbers 100,000 – 999,999

- **Target WPM:** 60+

Vocabulary
☐ **capital** 首都   ☐ **population** 人口   ☐ **approximately** およそ、約   ☐ **roughly** だいたい、およそ   ☐ **according to ~** 〜によると   ☐ **survey** 調査、アンケート
☐ **conduct** 実施する、実行する   ☐ **10,000** 1万 ten thousand   ☐ **100,000** 10万 one hundred thousand   ☐ **million** 100万   ☐ **billion** 10億   ☐ **trillion** 1兆
☐ **substantial** かなりの、相当な   ☐ **rapid** 急激な   ☐ **steady** 安定した、しっかりした
☐ **moderate** ほどほどの、適度な   ☐ **slight** ほんの僅かの、極めて少量の

DOWNLOAD 18

Example

Tokyo is the capital of Japan, and one of the largest cities in the world. In 2018, the population of Tokyo was approximately 13,800,000. This is roughly 10.9 percent of Japan's total population of 126.4 million.

There are also many pets in Tokyo. According to a survey conducted in 2011 and 2012, there are about 600,000 dogs and over 1,100,000 cats in Tokyo.

🔊 | Shadowing and Overlapping

For self-study or in-class practice, listen to the audio, do shadowing and overlapping of the example. Practice the passage until you can say it smoothly.

✍ | Create Your Own

Make a list of the numbers you want to use in your passage and practice.

Example

① 768

② How do you read it?　Seven hundred sixty-eight

③ What is the significance of the number? It is the number of universities in Japan as of 2018.

① (Your number) _____.

② How do you read it? _____.

③ What is the significance of the number? _____

_____.

④ (Your number) _____.

⑤ How do you read it? _____.

⑥ What is the significance of the number? _____

_____.

⑦ (Your number) _____.

⑧ How do you read it? _____.

⑨ What is the significance of the number? _____.

Sample Topics

● Your hometown and its population and other data

● An area of science you are interested in that uses large numbers

● Your living expenses and / or how you spend your money each month

🗣 | Training

Step 1: Fill in the blanks on the left.

Step 2: Practice reading numbers smoothly.

Step 3: Write your number on a place of paper.

Step 4: Make groups of three or four students.

Step 5: Introduce your number to your group. Do not read the text.

🗣 | Advanced Practice 1: Reading numbers smoothly

Read the following sentences with numbers without stopping.

1. The total number of students at TUS is about 19,800*.

   *nineteen thousand eight hundred

2. The population of Noda city is approximately 153,000*.

   *one hundred and fifty-three thousand

3. Company A's annual car production in 2018 was 9,775,324*.

   *nine million seven hundred and seventy-five thousand three hundred and twenty-four.

🗣 | Advanced Practice 2: Reading large numbers

1. Make groups of four or five students.

2. Each student has 2 or 3 cards or pieces of paper.

3. Write a large number (any number above 1,000) on the front side of each card.

4. Write down how to read the number on the back of the card.

5. Show the front side of the card to your group.

6. The first person to say the number correctly gets the card.

7. Take turns.

8. The student who gets the most cards wins.

Presentation Skills + Useful Expressions

When you talk about changes, try to use descriptive words to give your message more impact.

◆ **Useful Expressions and Collocations**
Listen to the audio and practice speaking.

1. a substantial amount / a substantial drop / substantial gain / substantial risk / substantial loss

2. rapid change / rapid expansion / rapid recovery / rapid increase / rapid decrease

3. steady flow / steady increase / steady decrease / steady growth / steady expansion

4. slight increase / slight decrease / slight chance / slight adjustment / slight difference

Unit | 13

Comparison

- **Main Objective:** Be able to use comparatives
- **Advanced Objective:** Be able to use the superlative
- **Target Expressions:**
    - A is ~er than B
    - A is more ~ than B
    - A is the ~est (in / among / of) ...
    - A is the most ~ (in / among / of) ...

- **Target WPM:** 60+

Vocabulary

☐ **laptop** ラップトップコンピュータ　　☐ **tablet** タブレット　　☐ **just** ただ、単純に
☐ **browse** インターネットのサイトの閲覧　　☐ **the web** ウェブ［インターネット］　　☐ **lean towards ~** ～をより好む　　☐ **physical** 実際の（現物として存在する）

原形－比較級－最上級

light – lighter – lightest

cheap – cheaper – cheapest

powerful – more powerful – the most powerful

(Usually a word with more than two syllables becomes more ~ / the most ~.)

 DOWNLOAD 19

Example

A: Which do you think I should get – a laptop or a tablet?

B: If you just need something to browse the web and check email, I'd recommend a tablet. They're lighter than laptops. They're cheaper, too.

A: Hmm... Actually, I was leaning towards a laptop. It's true that tablets are lighter, but I prefer typing on a physical keyboard. And sometimes I want a machine with a more powerful CPU.

🗣 | Shadowing and Overlapping

For self-study or in-class practice, listen to the audio, do shadowing and overlapping of the example. Practice the passage until you can say it smoothly.

📝 | Create Your Own

Create a roleplay. Student A asks Student B for a recommendation about something. Then Student B tells Student A his / her opinion and supports it with reasons.

Finally, Student A responds to Student B's recommendation. Student A can either accept or reject Student B's recommendation, but give reasons for your response using comparatives.

A: Which do you think (I should get / is better) — _____ or

_____ ?

B: If you _____, I'd recommend _____.

It's / They're (比較) _____.

A: _____

_____ .

Sample Topics
A. Physical books vs. Digital books
B. Glasses vs. Contact lenses
C. Living in a city vs. Living in the country
D. Traveling with friends vs. Traveling on your own
E. Working at a big company vs. Working at a start-up

🗣️ | Training

Step 1: Fill in the blanks on the left.

Step 2: Practice reading the roleplay out loud.

Step 3: Practice speaking without looking at what you wrote. If you forget, it is OK to glance at what you wrote.

Step 4: Make pairs and practice the two roleplays you and your partner created.

Step 5: Choose one roleplay to perform as a pair.

Step 6: Create a group of 2-3 pairs. Perform roleplays in front of your group. Try not to read the text.

🗣️ | Advanced Practice 1: Writing your own sentences

Fill in the gaps in the following sentences on your own. Work with a partner or in a group. Share your answers and read them aloud.

1. Dogs (are / have) _____ than cats.

2. Japan (is / has) _____than India.

3. The moon (is / has) _____ than the earth.

4. Tokyo is the _____ city in Japan.

5. Mathematics is one of the most _____ subjects of all.

🧑‍🤝‍🧑 | Advanced Practice 2: Describing more details

Use one of the sample topics (A-E) from the Create Your Own section (p. 60) and compare the two things. Compare them on three different points.

For example, say you choose topic A. You should compare physical and digital books with regard to: convenience, portability, price, etc.

Choose one topic and come up with three different comparison points. Here is an example of how to organize your speech. It helps to copy this example, or use a different structure. You can change words in the brackets.

Sample Format

I'd like to compare (physical books) and (digital books).
I'll compare them based on (convenience), (readability), and (price).

First, let me talk about (convenience). _____

_____

Next, I'll talk about (readability).

_____

Finally, I'd like to look at (price).

_____

Presentation Skills + Useful Expressions

◆ How to stress words

In English, it is important to know which part of a word has the strongest stress.

If you do not use the correct stress, your audience will have a difficult time understanding your presentation.

1. **Practice pronouncing syllables in uppercase strongest.**

LAPtop

TABlet

recomMEND

KEYboard

POWerful

ACTually

maCHINE

cpU

2. **When words end with -tion, -ian, and -ic(al) the syllable just before it is stressed.**

recomMEND - recommenDAtion

coLLAborate - collaboRAtion

SYstem - systeMAtic

aNAlysis - anaLYtical

Unit | 14

Agreeing and Disagreeing

- **Main Objective:** Agree and disagree effectively
- **Advanced Objective:** Disagree effectively with softening expressions
- **Target Grammar:** Agreeing
- **Target Expressions:**
    - Agreeing

      I agree. / I agree with your statement.

    - Disagreeing

      I disagree. / I can't agree with you. / I have a different opinion. / I see it differently.

    - Disagreeing politely

      I'm afraid, ... / I'm sorry but, ... / That doesn't sound right to me. / Sorry, but I don't think I can agree with you. / I have a different view. / I see it differently. / That doesn't seem ... to me.

- **Target WPM:** 60+

Vocabulary

☐ **continue** 継続する、続ける   ☐ **start over** 最初からやり直す   ☐ **have a point** 的を射ている、一理ある   ☐ **totally** 完全に   ☐ **regret** 後悔する   ☐ **reject** 拒絶する、断る ☐ **compulsory** 必須の   ☐ **firmly** 固く、きっぱりと   ☐ **positively** 明確に、きっぱりと ☐ **completely** 完全に

DOWNLOAD 21

Example

A: You said that you wanted to continue, but I don't think we can complete this research project. We should pick a new topic and start over.

B: You have a point, but I can't agree with your suggestion. We've already spent three weeks doing research. We only have two more weeks until our report is due. There's not enough time to start over now. Let's ask the professor for advice.

🗨️ | Shadowing and Overlapping

For self-study or in-class practice, listen to the audio, do shadowing and overlapping of the example. Practice the passage until you can say it smoothly.

✍️ | Create Your Own

Do you agree or disagree with the following statement? Use specific reasons and examples to support your opinion.

"Learning art and literature should be compulsory for students majoring in science."

Your Passage

I (agree / disagree) with the statement.

_____

_____

_____

_____

🔊 | Training

Step 1: Write your own passage.
Step 2: Practice reading your sentences out loud.

Step 3: Practice speaking without looking at what you wrote. If you forget, it is OK to glance at what you wrote.

Step 4: Make groups of three or four students.

Step 5: Introduce your opinion in front of your group. Do not read the text.

Advanced Practice 1: Hearing others' opinions

Come up with a statement that you would like to hear other students' opinions on. Write down your statement in your notebook. Make pairs. Student A makes a statement and Student B <u>agrees or disagrees</u> with Student A's statement, and gives his / her reasons. Take turns.

Your statement _____

_____ .

Your partner's statement _____

_____ .

I (agree / disagree) with the statement.

_____

_____ .

Advanced Practice 2: Disagreeing politely

Make pairs. Student A makes a statement and Student B <u>disagrees</u> with Student A's statement <u>with some softening expressions (p. 64) and reasons for disagreeing</u>. Take turns.

▶ Sample Topics for Advanced Practice 1 & 2

1. Small classes are better than large classes.
2. Violent video games should be prohibited.
3. Education makes us happier.

DOWNLOAD 22

🏫 | Presentation Skills + Useful Expressions

Learn some emphatic expressions commonly used in presentations. Find the best combinations and connect 1~5 and A~E to make sentences. Listen to the audio and practice saying the completed expressions.

1. We deeply _____.

2. We strongly _____.

3. We totally _____.

4. We completely _____.

5. We firmly _____.

A. recommend he start writing his report soon
B. agree with what you said in the meeting
C. support the timely decision the school made
D. reject any recommendations from your side
E. regret that we were unable to accept your proposal

Answer keys: 1 - E, 2 - A, 3 - D, 4 - B, 5 - C

Unit | 15

Pros and Cons

- **Main Objective:** Talk about something objectively from both positive and negative points of view
- **Advanced Objective:** Talk about pros and cons in a logical flow using appropriate signposting words
- **Target Expressions:** Signposting

  Signposting words show readers the next direction of the argument and prepare them to follow the logic.

  ex. Although / Though / but / However / On the other hand / On the contrary / Whereas

- **Target WPM:** 70+

Vocabulary

□ **pros and cons**　賛否両論、良い点と悪い点、メリットとデメリット　　□ **objectively**　客観的に
□ **online**　ネット上の、オンラインの　　□ **whenever ~**　～の時はいつでも　　□ **opportunity**
機会、好機　　□ **interact with ~**　～と交流する　　□ **online discussion board**　オンラインの
（意見交換のための）掲示板　　□ **dynamics**　ダイナミクス、（複雑なものの）動態、在り方
□ **signposting**　道標、道しるべ、（翻って）文脈の転換点を示す言葉

 DOWNLOAD 23

> **Example**
>
> There are pros and cons of taking a college course online. In an online course you don't have to go to campus, and you can watch course videos whenever you want. This is very convenient. On the other hand, there isn't much opportunity to interact with your classmates, so some people might not like it. Although many courses have an online discussion board, the dynamics are very different from having a discussion in a classroom in real time.

🗣 | Shadowing and Overlapping

For self-study or in-class practice, listen to the audio, do shadowing and overlapping of the example. Practice the passage until you can say it smoothly.

✏ | Create Your Own

Choose one of the sample topics below, or use your own, and talk about the pros and cons of a topic of your choice.

Sample Topics
hosting the Olympic Games / social media / studying abroad / living in Tokyo / using plastic bottles / animal testing for drugs / English as a required subject

Your Passage

> There are pros and cons of _____ .
>
> (Pros)
>
> _____
>
> _____
>
> _____ .
>
> (Cons)
>
> On the other hand, _____
>
> _____
>
> _____ .

🔊 | Training

Step 1: Fill in the blanks on p. 69.

Step 2: Practice reading your sentences out loud.

Step 3: Practice speaking without looking at what you wrote. If you forget, it is OK to glance at what you wrote.

Step 4: Make groups of three or four students.

Step 5: Say your passage in front of your group. Don't read the text.

👥 | Advanced Practice

Short debate

① Choose a topic to debate from the sample topics on p. 69.

② Make groups of 4-6 students (preferably an even number).

③ Divide the group into two. One is the "pro" team and the other is the "con" team.

④ Have a 5-10 minute discussion in your group to come up with several good reasons to support your team's position.

⑤ Speaking order:

Pro team student 1 → Con team student 1 → Pro team student 2 → ...

⑥ When you want to disagree with the previous speaker's opinion, summarize what the previous speaker said first, and then state your own opinion and give your reasons.

To summarize, use some of the following expressions.

- Thank you for sharing your opinion. You've said that ~, but...

- Basically what you said was ~. However, ...

- You said ~, but actually ...

- You claimed that ~. However, ...

- It is true that ~. On the other hand, ...

>♟ | Pronunciation Tips: Contrasting

Using contrastive stress is a useful way to make a point with two opposing ideas. Contrasting is also used when you talk about (new / old) information. New information is always stressed, spoken louder and at a higher pitch. On the other hand, old information is unstressed. Read the following passage with contrastive stress on the expressions printed in bold.

> There are pros and cons of taking a college course online. **In an online course** you don't have to go to campus, and you can watch course videos whenever you want. This is very convenient. **On the other hand,** there isn't much opportunity to interact with your classmates, so some people might not like it. Although many courses have an **online discussion board**, the dynamics are very different from having a **discussion in a classroom** in real time.

🧑‍🏫 | Presentation Skills + Useful Expressions

Use contrasting expressions to reinforce the point you are making. Including dramatic contrasts will help you to keep the audience's attention. The following is the list of commonly used expressions.

◆ Useful Expressions

> **1.** ~. However, ~. / **2.** Some are ~. Others are ~. / **3.** We ~. Other people ~. /
> **4.** ~ years ago, ~. Nowadays, ~. / **5.** Nothing ~. / **6.** Instead of just ~, why don't we ~. / **7.** It's not a question of ~. It's a question of ~.
>
> <Or simply use contrasting words>
> **1.** online - face to face / **2.** east - west / **3.** Asia - Europe - the US /
> **4.** now - later / **5.** public - private / **6.** rising - falling / **7.** growing - shrinking

Unit | 16

Explaining Concepts

- **Main Objective:** Introduce concepts or words new to the listeners
- **Advanced Objective:** Use metaphors / analogies to help listeners' understanding
- **Target Expressions:**

    <Concept A> is like <Concept B>

    <Concept A> is similar to <Concept B>

    - Just like A, B (is / does) ~

    - A is the exact opposite of B

    - For example,

    - A is different from B in that ~

- **Target WPM:** 70+

Vocabulary

☐ **major** 専攻　☐ **official** 正式な　☐ **study group** 勉強会、学習グループ　☐ **spend** 費やす　☐ **lead** 率いる、指導する　☐ **research paper** 研究論文　☐ **relate to ~** ～に関連する　☐ **field** 分野、学術分野　☐ **get to know each other** （お互いを）知り合う

DOWNLOAD 25

Example

At Japanese universities, just like universities in many countries around the world, students have a major, but most students also join a zemi. A zemi is like an official study group. Students spend a lot of time studying with the professor who leads the zemi. For example, students gather on a regular basis and read research papers and make presentations. These are usually about topics related to the professor's field of research. Students in a zemi get to know each other and the professor quite well.

🗣 | Shadowing and Overlapping

For self-study or in-class practice, listen to the audio, do shadowing and overlapping of the example. Practice the passage until you can say it smoothly.

📝 | Create Your Own

Choose an interesting word or concept from books or web pages. Select one that other classmates might not know much about. If you have no idea or could not find a good one, use one of the sample topics below. Do more research on the topic by searching the Internet. When you explain the topic to your peers, use metaphors / analogies (something similar that your audience knows) if possible. You can say A (unfamiliar word / concept) is like B (something similar and familiar to your audience).

Sample Topics
Space elevator, Turkish Delight, Atoll, Haka, Mistletoe, Lederhosen, Okonomiyaki, Petanque, Cricket, Gateball, Kabaddi, etc.

Your Passage

① I'd like to introduce a (Japanese / Vietnamese / Chinese / new) word / concept,

_____.

② _____ is like _____

_____.

③ For example, _____

_____.

♪ | Training

Step 1: Fill in the blanks on p. 73.

Step 2: Practice reading your sentences out loud.

Step 3: Practice speaking without looking at what you wrote. If you forget, it is OK to glance at what you wrote.

Step 4: Make groups of three or four students.

Step 5: Introduce the concept or the word of your choice in front of your group. Don't read the text.

👥 | Advanced Practice: Using metaphors/analogies

Choose one or more concepts from the list of Sample Topics. Come up with a simple metaphor/analogy and an explanation.

Example

<Osechi>

Osechi is like Christmas dinner. Osechi is traditional Japanese food served at the new year. Just as people celebrate Christmas with a traditional Christmas dinner in the West, Japanese people celebrate New Year with Osechi.

<   >

_____

<   >

_____

👤 | Reading Tips: Contrasting

Read in chunks. When you read a sentence, make sure that you pay attention to chunks of meaning. You cannot cut a sentence or pause in the middle of a meaning chunk. The passage below is cut into meaning chunks. When you read, do not stop in the middle of the meaning chunks.

Common places where you can cut a sentence or make a pause are:
- after commas and periods
- after the subject (when you want to emphasize the subject)
- before conjunctions
- before relatives (who, which, where, when what, that, etc.)
- before prepositions
- before to infinitives

At Japanese universities, / just like at universities in many countries around the world, / students have a major, / but most students also join a zemi. /

A zemi / is a bit like an official study group. / Students spend a lot of time studying with the professor / who leads the zemi. /

For example, / students gather on a regular basis / and read research papers / and make presentations. / These are usually about topics related to the professor's field of research. /

Students in a zemi / get to know each other and the professor quite well.

Presentation Skills

In a presentation, your ability to chunk your speech appropriately is quite important. It helps make your speech clearer and easier to understand. Also, even if you are not a fluent speaker, chunking words will make your speech sound more natural and effective.

As you practiced in the Reading Tips section, apply the chunking rules to the passage (refer to Your Passage section) you created earlier in the lesson (p. 73) and practice reading it.

Unit | 17

Explaining a Process

- **Main Objective:** Explain a process, step-by-step
- **Advanced Objective:** Use transitions to show the flow of the process
- **Target Expressions:**
    - I'm going to (explain / talk about) how to ~,
    - After that
    - After -ing
    - Then
    - Next

- **Target WPM:** 70+

Vocabulary

□ boil　沸騰させる、ゆでる　　□ lid　蓋　　□ halfway　途中、半分、半ばまで　　□ remove　取り除く　　□ packet　袋、包み　　□ contain　含む、包含する　　□ flavoring　調味料、味付け、香料　　□ empty　（動）中身を空ける　（形）空の　　□ pour in　注ぎ込む　　□ stir　混ぜる、かき混ぜる

DOWNLOAD 26

Example

I'm going to explain how to make instant ramen.

First, boil some water.

Next, open the cup lid halfway, and remove the packet containing the flavoring powder. Open it, and empty the powder onto the dry noodles.

After that, pour in enough boiling water to cover the noodles completely.

Then close the lid and wait three minutes.

Finally, remove the lid completely, and stir the noodles with some chopsticks. Your ramen is now ready to eat. Enjoy! But be careful, it's hot!

🗨 | Shadowing and Overlapping

For self-study or in-class practice, listen to the audio, do shadowing and overlapping of the example. Practice the passage until you can say it smoothly.

🗒 | Create Your Own

Choose one of the sample topics from the list below or use your own. Assume that you are talking to someone on the phone, so that you cannot use gestures to explain the details of the process. Try to explain every step of the process verbally. The exact number of steps in your process is not important.

Sample Topics

How to cook your favorite dish (simple recipe) / How to make rice balls / How to make a good presentation / How to use a public bath in Japan / How to choose a personal computer / How to take a good selfie / How to choose a major / How to become a successful student at TUS

Your Passage

① I'm going to explain how to _____.

② First, _____

_____.

③ Next, _____

_____.

④ After that _____

_____.

⑤ Then, _____

_____ .

⑥ Finally, _____

_____ .

♪ | Training

Step 1: Fill in the steps on p. 77 and above.

Step 2: Practice reading your sentences out loud.

Step 3: Practice speaking without looking at what you wrote. If you forget, it is
OK to glance at what you wrote.

Step 4: Make groups of three or four students.

Step 5: Say your passage in front of your group. Don't read the text.

👥 | Advanced Practice

Group challenge

Make a group of 5 or 6 students. The teacher assigns the group a topic from the list of Sample Topics or creates his / her own topic for the group. The group has 10 minutes to prepare. As a group, students discuss what the steps are. After that, each student is assigned one step to present. For example, Student A → step ① , Student B → step ② , etc. If there are more steps than students, some students will present more than one step. Finally, the group presents the process to the class. Make sure that each student speaks at least once.

Reading Tips: Content words and function words

In English, words can be put into two categories: content words and function words. In general, content words are categorized into: nouns, verbs, adjectives, and adverbs. Function words include pronouns, be-verbs, articles, prepositions, and conjunctions, etc. Content words are pronounced louder and clearer than function words. Function words are usually pronounced much weaker, and as a result they often contain sound changes and linking.

In the following passage, practice reading words written in a smaller font intentionally weak. Also, put extra stress on the words in bold letters.

I'm going to explain how to make instant ramen.

First, boil some water.

After that, open the cup lid halfway, and remove the packet containing the flavoring powder. Open it and empty the powder onto the dry noodles.

After that, pour in enough boiling water to cover the noodles completely.

Then close the lid and wait three minutes.

Finally, remove the lid completely, and stir the noodles with some chopsticks.

Your ramen is now ready to eat.

Enjoy! But be careful, it's hot!

Presentation Skills

Pausing is an important technique for helping your audience understand the content of your speech clearly. In the following example, sentences are cut into chunks of meaning by creating new lines. Make sure that you pause briefly at the end of every line where a - appears.

Practice Reading Aloud

I'm goin(g) to explain -
how to make instan(t) ramen. -
Firs(t), -
boil some water. -
Nex(t), -
open the cu(p) li(d) halfway, -
an(d) remove the packe(t) containin(g) the flavorin(g) powder. -
Open_i(t), -
an(d) empty the powder onto the dry noodles. -
After tha(t), -
pour_in enough boilin(g) water -
to cover the noodles completely. -
Then close the li(d) -
an(d) wai(t) three minutes. -
Finally, -
remove the li(d) completely, -
an(d) stir the noodles with some chopsticks. -
Your ramen is now ready to ea(t). -
Enjoy! -
Bu(t) be careful, -
it's ho(t)!

Unit | 18

Explaining Graphs, Charts and Tables 1

- **Main Objective:** Explain information contained in graphs and charts
- **Advanced Objective:** Summarize the main idea of graphs and charts
- **Target Expressions:**
    - Let's have a look at this (graph / chart).
    - This (graph / chart) shows ~.
    - The horizontal (x) axis (is / shows) ~, and the vertical (y) axis (is / shows) ~.
    - In this (graph / chart), the independent variable is ~, and the dependent variable is ~.
    - As you can see from this (graph / chart), ~.
    - Over the period of ~, A (increased / decreased) ~.
    - So we can say the relationship between A and B is ~.

- **Target WPM:** 80+

Vocabulary
□ line graph　折れ線グラフ　　□ pie chart　パイチャート　　□ seasonal　季節の
□ variation　変動、多様性　　□ variable　変数　　□ milk fat　乳脂肪　　□ horizontal　水平
の　　□ vertical　垂直の　　□ axis　軸　　□ gradually　徐々に　　□ increase　増加する、増
える　　□ decrease　減少する、減る　　□ peak / peak out　（動）最も高くなる、頂点に達する
（名）頂点　　□ level out　同じレベルになる（一定の数値で安定する）　　□ drop　下降する、落ちる、
減少する　　□ (and) vice versa　（そして）逆もまた同様である

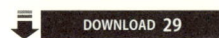
Example

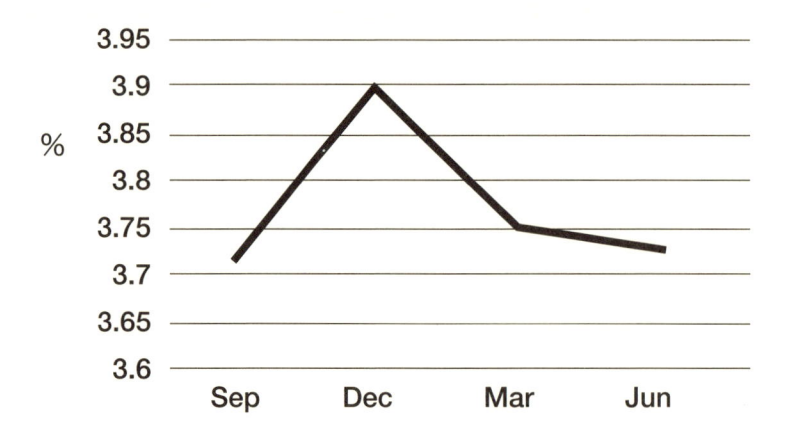

Seasonal Variation of Milk Fat

Let's have a look at this chart. It shows the seasonal variation of milk fat in milk. The horizontal axis shows the months of the year, and the vertical axis shows the milk fat percentage. From September to December, the percentage gradually increases. It peaks at 3.9 percent in December, and then decreases steadily from December to March. From March to June it levels out. From this chart we can see that milk fat percentage drops as the weather gets colder and vice versa.

Shadowing and Overlapping

For self-study or in-class practice, listen to the audio, do shadowing and overlapping. Practice the passage until you can say it smoothly.

Maximum Moisture Carrying Capacity of Air

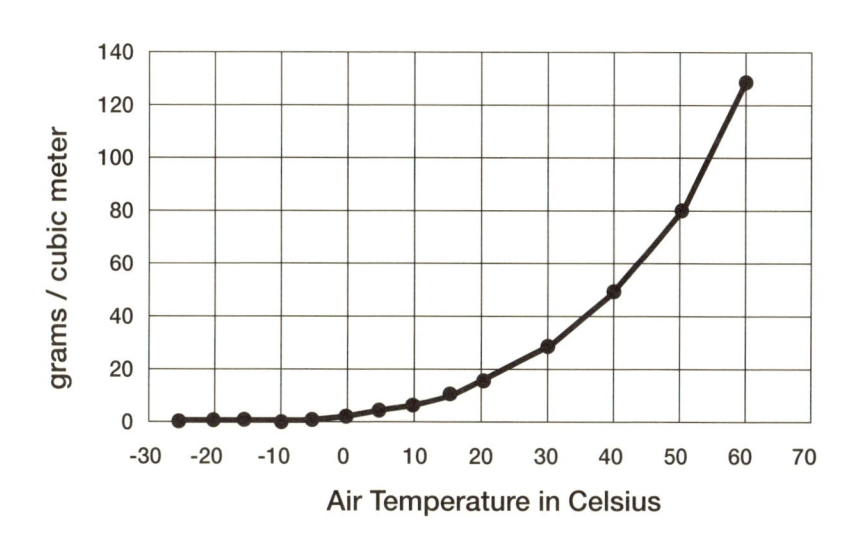

Vocabulary

☐ cubic meters = m3（立法メートル）　　☐ grams / cubic meter (grams per cubic meter)　　☐ Celsius = ℃　摂氏〜度　　☐ A is proportional to B　A は B に比例する

Your Passage

① Let's have a look at _____.

② It shows _____

　_____.

③ The horizontal (x) axis shows _____, and

　the vertical (y) axis shows _____

_____.

④ As you can see, the lower the temperature, _____

_____, and vice versa.

_____.

⑤ In the chart, at minus 20 degrees Celsius, _____

and at 40 degrees Celsius, _____.

⑥ From this chart we can see that _____

_____.

🗣 | Training

Step 1: Fill in the blanks on p. 83 and above.

Step 2: Practice reading your sentences out loud.

Step 3: Practice speaking without looking at what you wrote. If you forget, it is OK to glance at what you wrote.

Step 4: Make groups of three or four students.

Step 5: Practice explaining the graph in front of your group.

Advanced Practice

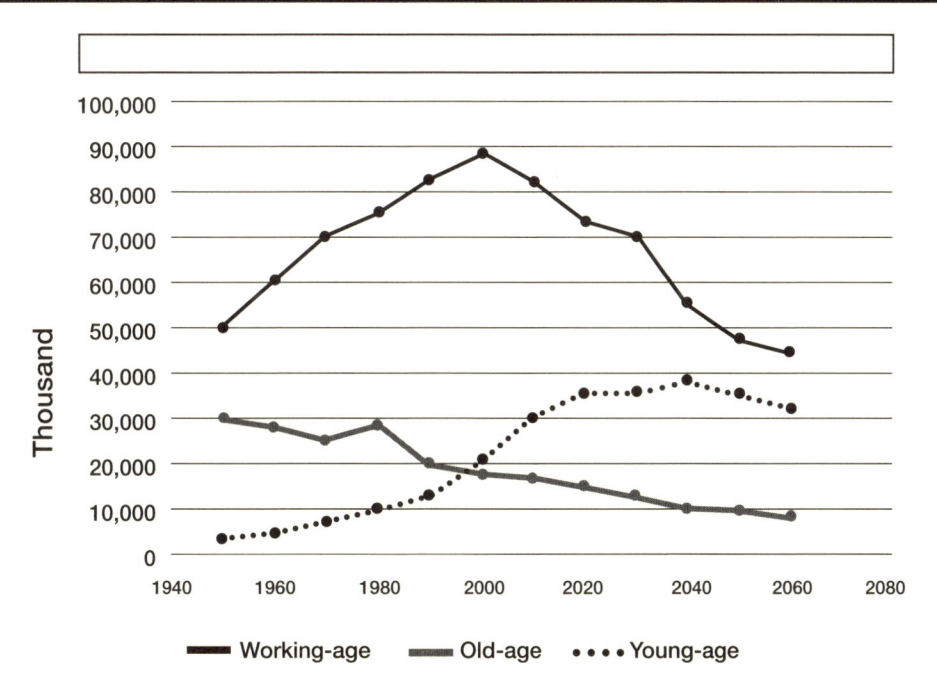

| Working-age | Old-age | •••• Young-age |

The graph on the above shows the percentage of the population that is of Working-age (age 15-64), Old-age (age 65 and over), and Young-age (age under 15).

◆ Vocabulary & Expressions

go up / increase / rise

go down / decrease / decline / drop

A reached its (highest / lowest) point in (year) at (%).

After 2060, it is (likely that / possible that) ~

1. Explain each country's data (major highs and lows and implications).
2. Compare the two lines and come up with your own conclusion.
3. Think of a title for the graph that reflects your conclusion.

_____

4. Predict what is likely to happen in the future.

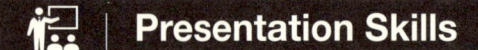 **Presentation Skills**

➡ Tips for Explaining Graphs

1. After giving a brief introduction of the graph, give your audience some time just to look at the graph and think. Do not start explaining the graph immediately.

2. When you explain the graph, do not just talk about the lines. Rather, talk more about the (implications / conclusions) you can draw from the graph.

3. Repeat key points several times so that the audience does not miss the most important message you are trying to convey.

4. Do not rush your explanations of important (numbers / results / implications). People in the audience may need some time to understand what you are saying.

Unit | 19

Explaining Graphs, Charts and Tables 2

- **Main Objective:** Explain information contained in graphs, charts and tables
- **Advanced Objective:** Summarize the main idea of the graphs, charts and tables
- **Target Expressions:**
    - Let's take a look at this (bar / pie / line / waterfall / Gantt) chart.
    - Please take a look at page 3 of your (handouts / textbook).
    - This table contains data for ~.
    - As you can see in the column headings, ...
    - The right column shows ... / As you can see in the left column, ...
    - From the data, (it looks like / it appears that) ...
    - As A increases, B (decreases / also increases).
    - So we can say the (relationship / correlation) between A and B is ...
    - A is (proportional / inversely proportional) to B

- **Target WPM:** 80+

Vocabulary

☐ average 平均　　☐ rainfall 降雨量　　☐ throughout ～を通して　　☐ indicate 示す
☐ approximately およそ、約　　☐ in part because ひとつには～の理由で　　☐ a large majority 大多数　　☐ minority 少数　　☐ the rest 残り　　☐ proportional 比例している
☐ inversely proportional 反比例している　　☐ correlation 相関関係

Example

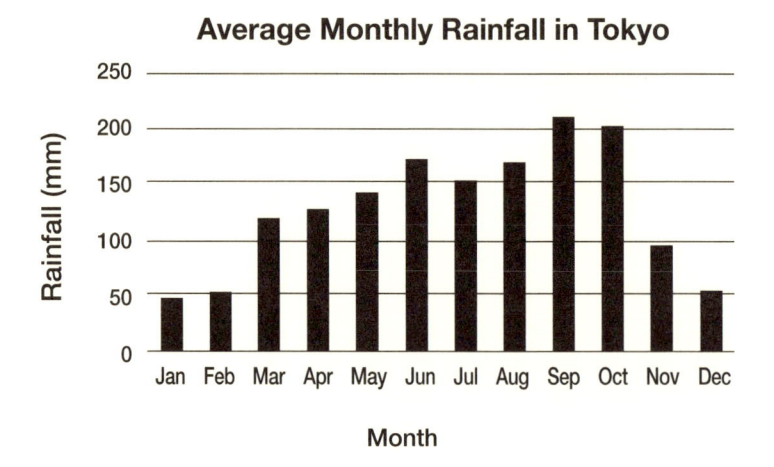

Please take a look at the screen. This bar chart shows the average monthly rainfall in Tokyo throughout the year. Longer bars indicate more rain, and shorter bars indicate less. As you can see, December, January and February are the driest months, with approximately 50 mm of rain each month. On the other hand, more than 150 mm of rain falls monthly from June through October. September and October are the wettest months in part because that is the peak of typhoon season.

👤 | Shadowing and Overlapping

For self-study or in-class practice, listen to the audio, do shadowing and overlapping of the example. Practice the passage until you can say it smoothly.

📝 | Create Your Own

Find out where your classmates come from. Ask "Where are you from?" After finding out the numbers, fill the table. Calculate percentage for each category and divide the pie chart accordingly.

Area	Number of Students	Percentage
Greater Tokyo		
North Kanto		
Tokai		
Kansai / Chugoku		
Kyushu / Shikoku / Okinawa		
Hokkaido		
International		
Total		100

Your Passage

① Let's have a look at this pie chart and the table.

② It shows _____

_____.

③ The majority _____, and the rest

_____.

④ In part, this is because _____

_____.

⑤ I'm from _____, so I belong to the group representing

_____ % of students in this class.

⑥ From this chart we can say that _____

_____.

🔊 | Training

Step 1: Fill in the blanks on p. 89 and above.

Step 2: Practice reading your sentences out loud.

Step 3: Practice speaking without looking at what you wrote. However, it is OK to look at the graph. If you forget, it is OK to glance at what you wrote.

Step 4: Make groups of three or four students.

Step 5: Practice explaining the graph in front of your group.

Memo

🗣️ Advanced Practice: Choosing your focus

Find some interesting facts from the table below and tell them to your peers.

Largest Countries in the World

Country	Rank	Area (sq. km)	Population	Population Density (per sq. km)
Russia	1	17,125,191	146,877,088	8.6
Canada	2	9,984,670	37,242,571	3.7
United States	3	9,796,742	327,167,434	33.4
China	4	9,596,961	1,403,500,365	146.2
Brazil	5	8,515,867	210,147,125	24.7
Australia	6	7,692,024	25,234,600	3.3
India	7	3,287,263	1,324,171,354	402.8

1. Read the table carefully and choose some interesting facts you noticed from the table.

2. Decide your conclusion and write a topic sentence.

   Topic sentence: _____

   _____ .

3. Think of a title for the table that reflects your conclusion. The title of the table 'Largest Countries in the World' suggest the content of the table, but not what it indicates. Depending on the topic of your presentation, you can create your own title such as 'India is one of the most densely populated countries in the world.' Try and be more specific than 'Largest Countries in the World'.

   Your title of the table: _____

   _____ .

4. Make sure that your topic sentence and the title you created are consistent.

5. Practice saying numbers that are important to support your conclusion.

6. Share some interesting facts and your conclusions with your peers.

Presentation Skills

When you give a presentation, there are many things that you need to pay attention to. One of the most important things is delivery. It includes eye contact, voice, posture and gestures.

Eye-contact Do not just read from your prepared text. Make eye-contact with your audience. Relax and smile.

Voice If you speak too softly, your audience will not be able to hear what you are saying. Make sure that your voice is loud enough for everyone in the room to hear. Also, speak slowly and clearly.

Posture Stand up straight with your arms relaxed at your side. Do not lean against the wall or a desk.

Gestures If you stand still and never move during the presentation, it could be boring. Gestures and movements can make your presentation more interesting and easier to follow, but they should have meaning. Movements and gestures that are not related to what you are saying are distracting rather than helpful.

Unit | 20

Review Unit

- **Main Objective:** Prepare a maximum 5-minute presentation on something you are interested in. Prepare an outline of your presentation, chart and slides (if necessary). Follow tips and the steps introduced in the Presentation Skills section in each unit.
- **Advanced Objective:** Give a presentation clearly, effectively and passionately with good eye contact, gesture, and posture.

Presentation Skills

Preparing for a presentation requires a lot of time and work. So students should start preparing for their presentation at least a month before their actual delivery.

Prepare a 5-minute presentation. When planning your presentation think about how much information you will need for your presentation to last around 5 minutes.

1. Decide a topic and do some research.
2. Decide the main message you want to (convey / introduce) to the audience.
3. Decide the presentation title.
4. Decide the main content of the presentation (maximum three parts).
5. Prepare the text and slides for the beginning part of the presentation.
   Refer to Units 1, 2, 3 and 4 for expressions and tips.
6. Prepare the text, slides and charts for the main body of the presentation.
   Refer to Units 5, 6, 11, 12, 13, 14, 15, 16 and 17 for expressions and tips. Refer to Units 18 and 19 for expressions and tips for charts.
7. Prepare the text and slides for the conclusion of the presentation.
   Refer to Units 7, 8 and 9 for expressions and tips.
8. If you are making a group presentation, decide who is going to be responsible for which part of the presentation.

9. Once you have prepared the text, practice reading aloud and make sure the entire presentation fits in 5 minutes plus 2 minutes for Q&A for individual presentation. For group presentation, 12 minutes plus 3 minutes for Q&A.

10. Practice! Practice! Practice!
It is strongly recommended that you practice your presentation until you can explain the content without looking at your script.

11. Record your voice and listen. Are your volume, speed and pausing easy for listeners to understand?

12. Watch some good TED videos and other popular speech videos, learn effective use of pauses and gestures.

13. Rehearse. Ask some friends to listen to your presentation and get some feedback for further improvement.

14. Film yourself while practicing. Do you make enough eye-contact with your audience? Do you look confident?

15. Copy the tables on pp. 95-96 and refer to them if you forget your lines.

Your Presentation Title

Introduction (Refer to Units 1, 2, 3 and 4)

	Time (min)	Key Phrases
Self-introduction		
Purpose of the presentation		
Outline		

Main Body (Refer to Units 5, 6, 11, 12, 13, 14, 15, 16 and 17)

Topics	Time (min)	Key Phrases
1.		
2.		
3.		

Chart / Graph / Table (if needed) (Units 18 and 19)

Conclusion (Refer to Units 7, 8 and 9)

	Time (min)	Key Phrases
Let the audience know that the talk is about to end		
Restate the main points Thank the audience		
Q&A		

==

◆ Feedback Sheet

Scores: 1= Practice more!   2 = OK   3 = Good Job!

Name / Group of the presenter

_____

	Score	Comments
1. Introduction		
2. Main body		
3. Graphs / charts		
4. Conclusion		
5. Q&A		
6. Volume		
7. Eye contact		
8. Was the message clear?		
Total Score		

Feedback by _____

Suggestions for managing the presentations

★ If it is a relatively small class of less than 30 students,
  0:00-60:00
1. Divide the class into groups of 4-5 students.
2. Each student gives a presentation in front of his / her group.
3. Listeners give feedback (see the feedback sheet above) to speakers.
  60:00-90:00
4. Choose the best speaker of the group.
5. If time allows, all the best speakers give their presentation in front of the entire class.

6. If not, depending on the time left, one or two best speakers give their presentation in front of the class.

★ If the class has more than 40 students,
0:00-70:00
1. Divide the class into groups of 6-7 students.
2. Each student gives a presentation in front of his / her group.
3. Listeners give feedback (see the feedback sheet on the left) to speakers.
70:00-90:00
4. Each group chooses the best speaker in the group.
5. One of the best speakers gives his / her presentation in front of the class.

★ If it is a group presentation and the number of groups is less than 6,
0:00-70:00
1. Each group gives a presentation in front of the class.
70:00-90:00
2. Listeners give feedback to the group.
3. Vote for the best group.

About the author

Ms. Makiko Asaba is the co-founder and CEO at Q-Leap Inc, an educational service company specializes in English teaching. Ms. Asaba acquired a master's degree in TESOL (Teaching English to Speakers of Other Languages) from Columbia University Teachers College with the hope of contributing to English education in Japan. She has trained more than 5,000 Japanese executives and business professionals through corporate lessons. Her interests include business English and English for specific purposes (ESP) especially in the area of speaking.

浅場 眞紀子（あさば・まきこ）

　コロンビア大学ティーチャーズカレッジ英語教授法（TESOL）修士課程修了。 慶応義塾大学卒業後、米穀物メジャー Cargill、石油メジャー BP の外資 2 社に計 10 年トレーダー兼アナリストとして勤務。その間シカゴ、NY、ジュネーブに合計 3 年半駐在。ビジネスバックグラウンドと英語教授法の理論を組み合わせた企業研修を目指し、パートナーの愛場吉子と 2014 年に Q-Leap 株式会社（http://q-leap.co.jp/）設立。

　現在は企業研修、セミナー、その他大学、ビジネススクールなどで教壇に立つ他、コンテンツ作成も多方面で行っている。

　主な著書に、『[音声 DL 付] 話せる英語ドリル 300 文〜 Q-Leap 式！ 1 日 10 文で始める・続ける』『ビジネスがはかどる！ 英文 E メールハンドブック』（アルク）、『TOEIC テストスピーキング / ライティング総合対策』（旺文社）など。

Speaking Practice for Presenting in English
Tokyo University of Science English Listening and Speaking

● 2019 年 8 月 30 日　初版発行　●

● 著者 ●
Makiko Asaba（浅場 眞紀子）

Copyright © 2019 by Makiko Asaba

発行者　●　吉田尚志
発行所　●　株式会社　研究社
〒 102-8152　東京都千代田区富士見 2-11-3
●電話●営業 03-3288-7777（代）　編集 03-3288-7711（代）
●振替● 00150-9-26710
http://www.kenkyusha.co.jp/

KENKYUSHA
装丁　●　久保和正
組版・レイアウト ●　古正佳緒里
印刷所　●　研究社印刷株式会社
ISBN978-4-327-42200-4　C1082　Printed in Japan

本書のコピー、スキャン、デジタル化等の無断複製は、著作権法上での例外を除き、禁じられています。
また、私的使用以外のいかなる電子的複製行為も一切認められていません。落丁本、乱丁本はお取り替え致します。
ただし、古書店で購入したものについてはお取り替えできません。